LNER
THE LONDON AND NORTH
EASTERN RAILWAY
Paul Atterbury

SHIRE PUBLICATIONS
Bloomsbury Publishing Plc
PO Box 883, Oxford, OX1 9PL, UK
1385 Broadway, 5th Floor, New York, NY 10018, USA

E-mail: shire@bloomsbury.com
www.shirebooks.co.uk

SHIRE is a trademark of Osprey Publishing Ltd

First published in Great Britain in 2018

A catalogue record for this book is available from the British Library.

ISBN: PB 978 1 78442 272 1
        eBook 978 1 78442 270 7
        epDF 978 1 78442 269 1
        XML 978 1 78442 271 4

18 19 20 21 22   10 9 8 7 6 5 4 3 2 1

Typeset by PDQ Digital Media Solutions, Bungay, UK

Printed and bound in India by Replika Press Private Ltd

Shire Publications supports the Woodland Trust, the UK's leading woodland conservation charity. Between 2014 and 2018 our donations are being spent on their Centenary Woods project in the UK.

COVER IMAGE

Front cover: Detail from a 1920s LNER poster, 'Harrogate Pullman', designed by George Harrison. Back cover: LNER luggage label for the 'Flying Scotsman'.

TITLE PAGE IMAGE

This poster by Ladislas Freiwirth advertises the LNER route from London to Scotland.

CONTENTS PAGE IMAGE

Postcard depicting the 'Flying Scotsman', 1920s.

ACKNOWLEDGEMENTS

Images are acknowledged as follows:

Alamy, front cover; Andrew/Flickr Creative Commons, page 25; Getty Images, pages 1, 34, 35, 36, 45 (bottom), 62; Lisa Phillips, page 10; Mjirlam/Wikimedia Commons, page 21 (bottom); Science and Society Picture Library, pages 48 (bottom), 50 (top), 55; Tony Hisgett/Flickr Creative Commons, page 26.

All other illustrations are from the author's own collection.

ONDON & NORTH EASTERN R⌐
THE FLYING SCOTSMAN"

CONTENTS

THE GROUPING

A T THE END of the First World War, Britain's railways were in a parlous state. Years of heavy use and inadequate maintenance had taken a toll on a network that had been built by over a hundred private companies that ranged in size from the major players such as the Great Western, the Midland and the London and North Western to minor lines serving essentially local needs. Many of these companies were in financial difficulties, with a total deficit of over £40 million, partly because of the impact of the war, and partly because of the considerable duplication of routes and stations, the result of fierce competition between Victorian railway builders. During the war, the government had taken control of the

Postcard
depicting Great
Eastern Railway
4-4-0 Class T19
locomotive and
passenger train
crossing Trowse
swing bridge
near Norwich, in
about 1910.

Postcard
depicting North
British Railway
4-4-2 Class H
locomotive
crossing the
Forth Bridge in
about 1910.

railways, while stopping short of actual nationalisation, and this control continued into the immediate post-war years.

In 1920 Eric Geddes, the Minister of Transport and a former deputy general manager of the North Eastern Railway and First Lord of the Admiralty, was asked to put together a plan for the future of Britain's railways. His White Paper formed the basis of the Railways Act of 1921, known popularly as the Grouping Act, the essence of which was that the major railways should be brought together into large regional groups. The original proposal was for six or seven areas or groups, including a separate one for Scotland, but for the Act that was passed in August 1921 this was reduced to four with Scotland included, defined as the Great Western Railway (GWR), the Southern Railway (SR), the London, Midland and Scottish Railway (LMS) and the London and North Eastern Railway (LNER). These quickly became known as the Big Four. A subsequent Act in 1933 created the London Passenger Transport Board to operate the capital's transport network. Though the regional boundaries were clearly drawn, there was inevitably some overlap and some anomalies, usually the result of pre-Grouping partnerships. Obvious examples were the LNER's operation of the West Highland line to Mallaig, deep into LMS territory,

and the LMS's control of the former London, Tilbury and
Southend route eastwards from London into LNER territory.
However, the core separation was between the main routes
from London to Scotland, with the LMS having the West
Coast route, and the LNER the East. The Railways Act came
into force on 1 January 1923.

The main constituent companies of the LNER were the
Great Eastern Railway, the Great Central Railway, the North
Eastern Railway, the Great Northern Railway, the Hull and
Barnsley Railway, the North British Railway and the Great
North of Scotland Railway. The most important of these, the
GER, the GCR, the NER and the GNR, had themselves been
created by mergers and amalgamations during the previous
century, while the ambitious NBR was the largest railway in
Scotland. In addition, brought into the Group were many other
lesser lines, giving the LNER a route length of 6,590 miles and
making it the second-largest of the Big Four. The very long
list of subsidiary, leased and jointly operated lines included
a few independent companies, such as the Mid-Suffolk
Light Railway, and a large number of lines leased or worked
by the main constituent LNER railways. There were about
twenty-four of these, mostly either short connecting railways

or nominally independent local and branch lines. They ranged from minor or obscure companies, such as the NER's goods only Fawcett Depot Line, the GCR's North Lindsey Light Railway, the GNR's Stamford and Essendine Railway and the NBR's Lauder Light Railway, to substantial and sometimes important lines on the railway map, such as the GER's London and Blackwell Railway, the GNR's East Lincolnshire Railway, the NBR's Forth and Clyde Junction Railway and the Hull and Barnsley's South Yorkshire Junction Railway.

There were also over twenty jointly operated lines, mostly shared with the LMS. The largest of these were the 183-mile East Anglian network of the Midland and Great Northern Joint Railway which, though incorporated into the LNER in 1936, continued to be shared by the LNER and the LMS, and the 142-mile Cheshire Lines Committee. Other joint LNER and LMS lines were to be found in many parts of England and Scotland and included the Axholme Light Railway, the Dundee and Arbroath Railway, the Great Central and North Staffordshire Joint Railway, the Norfolk and Suffolk Joint Railway and the Tottenham and Hampstead Junction Railway. The LNER's route map ran from London to Glasgow, Edinburgh, Aberdeen and Elgin and included Leicester, Sheffield, Manchester and Carlisle, along with most of East Anglia and all of eastern England from the Thames to Newcastle and the Border. In London, the LNER's main termini were King's Cross, formerly GNR, Liverpool Street, formerly GER, Marylebone, formerly GCR and Fenchurch Street, formerly London and Blackwall Railway.

Postcard depicting King's Cross Station during the Great Northern Railway era, in about 1910.

SETTING UP THE BUSINESS

A T ITS FORMATION the LNER found that it had inherited over 7,000 steam locomotives, 20,000 carriages, around 30,000 freight vehicles, a small fleet of electric trains and steam and motor railcars, over forty passenger and freight ships, a number of river and lake steamers, over twenty hotels and a massive fleet of road vehicles, including 800 mechanical horse tractors. It had shares in bus and road transport companies, and there were over 2,500 stations and goods depots, along with thousands of other buildings, including warehouses, signal boxes, houses and cottages, engine sheds, workshops and offices. The LNER also took charge of docks and harbours in twenty places, the most important of which were Hull, Immingham, Harwich, Grimsby, Hartlepool and London, along with Leith and Aberdeen. There were also smaller wharves and piers all over the network and eight canals. Over 205,000 staff were employed, along with a large number of horses.

From the start, the LNER built a reputation for sound and careful but creative management. The chairman, William Whitelaw, came from the NBR and the deputy chairman, Lord Faringdon, came from the GCR, companies well known for their careful and thrifty behaviour. The chief general manager, Sir Ralph Wedgwood, and his assistant, Robert Bell, both came from the NER.

The main challenge facing the LNER was the integration into one company of many independent railways, large

and small. Many were well known as efficient and well-run companies that had been financially viable until the depredations of the First World War, and they were generally regarded with great loyalty by both staff and customers. The larger ones had successfully operated a great range of trains over a long period, which included main-line and secondary passenger traffic, commuter services, excursions and a significant freight business. In addition some ran a network of dining and sleeping cars, along with steamers and hotels. Some, such as the GNR, were already famous for the quality and originality of their publicity and had established a particular look, or image. The larger companies had also built their own locomotives and vehicles, often with distinctive and individual approaches to design, construction and operation.

It is a reflection of the management skills of the chairman, William Whitelaw, and the general manager, Sir Ralph

In 1925 the centenary of Britain's railways was widely celebrated, with the North East at the heart of it. Among the locomotives on display was the then brand new LNER Class U1 Beyer-Garrett freight locomotive, the most powerful steam locomotive ever to run in Britain.

Wedgwood, both of whom remained at the helm until 1938, and their Board, that integration into the new LNER took place both quickly and relatively smoothly. From the start there was an acceptance of the need to modernise the network and to unify the disparate working practices of the old independent companies, and at the same time to encourage innovation in all areas of activity. There was also a degree of practical co-operation with the LMS, the LNER's main rival. Competition over things like the key routes to Scotland, the design and performance of locomotives, the operation of freight services and publicity was generally seen as inevitable, but frequently beneficial, and jointly managed routes and buildings were usually operated in an efficient way. Competition was, in any case, a two-edged sword. While initially encouraged by the government and promoted in advertising and publicity, it was soon seen as counterproductive, and by the 1930s the Big Four were openly co-operating in many areas of activity, and particularly in the handling of freight. However, the real problem faced by the LNER was money. The LNER was always the least profitable of the Big Four, despite its large network. By contrast, the LMS accounted for 40 per cent of the total traffic turnover on Britain's railways between the wars, and so was able to centralise, standardise and modernise in a far more dramatic fashion. In 1923, the LNER, as Britain's major coal carrier, seemed well placed but within a couple of years coal was in a steep decline, not helped by long-lasting strikes and disputes. Likewise, the core industries of the North East – iron, steel and shipbuilding – crucial to the LNER's finances, also declined significantly from the mid-1920s. While there was some recovery in the 1930s, in real terms the LNER was never really a profitable company. The rural nature of much of its network also caused it to suffer increasingly from the expansion of road traffic for both passengers and freight. In 1903 there were 18,000 mechanically propelled vehicles of all types in Britain. By 1928 that figure had exceeded two million. Increasingly, traffic regulations, taxation and costings favoured the roads, the foundation of the uneven playing field that has blighted railway transport ever since. Fast, streamlined trains with luxury carriages and great publicity may have been the public face of the LNER but behind the scenes there was a large and underfunded company struggling to survive.

The LNER's route map reveals the complex and uneven nature of the company's activities. At its heart are the main lines radiating from the three major London termini, Marylebone, King's Cross and Liverpool Street and linking most of England and Scotland's most important towns and cities on the eastern half of Britain. In addition, joint operations and through carriages also took the LNER into places as diverse as Bristol, Exeter and Penzance, Gloucester, Cardiff and Swansea, Oxford, Reading and Southampton, Birmingham, Stafford, Chester and Liverpool, Penrith and Stranraer, and Perth and Inverness. Over 60 per cent of Britain's towns with a population of over 50,000 were directly served by the LNER or by lines in which it had a share. Many of these routes and connections also allowed for the extensive exchange of freight traffic. Coal carrying was the primary freight business, thanks to the LNER's access to the coalfields of the north Midlands, the North East

Leaflet
promoting an FA
Amateur Cup
football match,
with an early
version of the
LNER shield.

LONDON
AND
NORTH EASTERN
RAILWAY

Football Match at Ilford.

F.A. Amateur Cup
(4th Round)
KICK-OFF 3.15 p.m.

ILFORD
v.
LONDON CALEDONIANS

SATURDAY, MARCH 3,
1923.

RETURN TICKETS
AT
SINGLE FARES
Fractional parts of 1d. are charged as 1d.

WILL BE ISSUED TO

ILFORD

by any train due to leave the issuing stations not later than 3.0 p.m.

From BRENTWOOD, ROMFORD and intermediate stations, available for return the same day by any train after 4.0 p.m.

☞ *Tickets can be obtained in advance at the stations.*

Children under 3 years of age, free ; 3 and under 12, half-price. No luggage allowed. The tickets are not transferable, and will only be available on the date, by the trains, and at the stations named ; if used on any other date, by any other train, or at any other station than those named, the tickets will be forfeited, and the full ordinary fare charged. The Company give notice that tickets for this Excursion are issued at a reduced rate, and only on condition that the Company shall not be liable for any oss, damage, injury or delay to Passengers arising from any cause.

London, February, 1923.

1904/2/23   Printed at the Company's Works, Stratford.   3000/12

and southern Scotland. In between the main lines there is a dense network of cross-country, secondary and other minor routes, including a large number of largely rural branch lines. Many of these were built in the latter part of the nineteenth century to serve relatively remote and underpopulated regions, particularly in East Anglia, Lincolnshire, the Scottish borders and north-east Scotland, at a time when social and economic life was dependent upon the railway. By the 1920s many of these were uneconomic. Liverpool Street was at the centre of some of Britain's busiest commuter lines, serving Hertfordshire and Essex and there was also a busy suburban network centred on Edinburgh. All these varieties of routes required particular types of traffic, timetables, marketing and operation, and that was the daily challenge for the LNER's senior management in its three regional centres. In an average year the LNER carried 370 million people, 140 million tons of freight and 8 million livestock.

'This Year?' holiday brochure, 1924, showing an early version of the LNER shield.

The map also indicates the importance of shipping for the LNER's business and financial structure. Scheduled passenger and freight services were operated from Aberdeen, Leith, Newcastle, Middlesbrough, Hull, Immingham and Harwich, to Scandinavia, Germany, Holland, Belgium and France. Some of these routes, such as Leith to Dunkirk and Middlesbrough to Calais and Dieppe, seem to have been established by competitive independent companies of the pre-LNER era, yet they survived into the 1930s.

THE LNER IMAGE

When it was set up, the LNER inherited with its long list of constituent companies a great variety of names, house styles and liveries for stations and rolling stock. In 1923, after inspecting locomotives from the various constituent companies, the Board decided that apple green should be the standard colour for locomotives, and varnished teak the finish for carriages, and this quickly gave the new company a distinctive look. However, this livery was never universal and it was only generally applied to passenger tender locomotives. Many others, including freight locomotives and passenger tank locomotives were painted black, and from 1941 most LNER locomotives were painted black as a wartime economy measure. Famously, the streamlined A4 Pacific locomotives were painted silver or garter blue, with matching carriages. Station and building colours were established quite early as stone or cream with brown. From 1936 the brown was changed to a mid green, known as Buckingham Green. Among the first stations to be repainted in the new style were Leicester, Colchester, Ely, Lowestoft and Chesterfield. This colour scheme was maintained until the formation of British Railways and in many cases survived until the 1950s.

From its formation the LNER attempted to develop a unified image or house style that could be applied to everything from station name boards to stationery, but this was very uneven and inconsistent until the 1930s. For example, station name boards were initially brown and cream, sometimes with light letters on a dark ground,

Manchester district summer timetables, 1939, with LNER eye-shaped badge.

and sometimes the other way round. In the 1930s this changed to blue and white. The LNER logotype is also surprisingly inconsistent until the 1930s, with the letters usually in a variety of typefaces with serifs, either in blue or reversed out of blue or red.

Enamel direction sign, showing the standard LNER colours and badge of the late 1930s.

There was also a brief flirtation with an LNER monogram in an old-fashioned script style. In the mid-1930s, order began to be imposed on this chaos and the LNER, along with the other Big Four companies, made a big effort to give itself a much more unified modern image. While this was inspired partly by modern marketing ideas, it also indicated a more general awareness of increased competition and financial challenges.

This approach had been famously pioneered by Frank Pick for London Transport and so the LNER followed this route, and began to use a sans serif letter form close to that designed by Eric Gill, matched with a new LNER logotype with the letters reversed out of an eye-shaped solid colour. These changes, driven by the company's marketing manager, William Teasdale, and continued by his successor, Cecil Dandridge, reflected an increasing awareness of the need for modern marketing backed by an immediately recognisable image or, to use the contemporary term, brand. This drive towards a new image was also underlined by stations and structures being rebuilt in art deco modern styles, by streamlined locomotives and rolling stock and by dramatic and colourful posters by well-known artists and designers that promoted both routes and destinations and a broader concept of luxury travel. The LNER was actually an industrial company, with two-thirds of its income coming from freight, yet the image it took care to present to the public was about glamour, luxury, sophistication and modern high-speed travel.

LOCOMOTIVES

THROUGHOUT ITS TWENTY-FIVE-YEAR life, the LNER used over thirty types of steam locomotive. At its formation in 1923, it inherited from its constituent companies a great variety of locomotives of varying ages, qualities and performance, along with a number of major locomotive works, of which the most important were Doncaster, Darlington, Gorton and Stratford. However, the LNER's intention was always to build its own locomotive fleet, while retaining and if necessary rebuilding the best of those that it had inherited.

It was with this in mind that it appointed as its first Chief Mechanical Engineer Herbert Nigel Gresley. Born in 1876, Gresley joined the railway industry as an apprentice at the London & North Western's works at Crewe. His rise through the industry was rapid and in 1911 he took over from Henry Ivatt as Chief Mechanical Engineer for the Great Northern Railway, designing eleven locomotive types for that railway, many of which passed into the service of the LNER. Maintaining his attachment to large and mechanically refined locomotives, Gresley quickly made his mark at the LNER by developing the A1 class, which he had designed for the GNR in 1922. This class was made enduringly famous by the *Flying Scotsman*, and led to a succession of famous high-speed passenger locomotive classes, culminating in the famous streamlined A4 Pacifics, one of which, *Mallard*, captured in 1938 the world speed record for steam locomotives, which it still holds. Less well known but more important for the

Former Great Northern Railway Class K locomotive of 1909, serving as LNER Class D33 number 9864, crossing the Forth Bridge in about 1925.

financial stability of the LNER were a number of classes of freight locomotives, along with some experimental designs which pushed forward the technical development of the steam locomotive. In all, Gresley developed or designed about sixteen locomotive classes for the LNER, including some electric and diesel types, along with the famous articulated carriage sets used for both main-line express and suburban services. Knighted in 1936, Sir Nigel Gresley died in 1941.

Gresley was succeeded by Edward Thompson. Born in 1881, Thompson had both an industrial and a railway background, and started his railway career at the North Eastern Railway. After the Grouping he worked for the LNER, becoming workshop manager at Stratford works in 1930. It is well known that he and Gresley did not get on, having many disagreements about the technical development of the steam locomotive and in addition Thompson was a notably difficult man to work with. When Gresley died suddenly in 1941, the LNER Chief Mechanical Engineer post was initially offered to Oliver Bulleid, formerly Gresley's assistant and now the Southern Railway's CME. However, he turned the job down and the next candidate, the LMS's J.F. Harrison was considered too young. So, it came to Edward Thompson and he was the LNER's Chief Mechanical Engineer until his retirement in 1946. Famous for redesigning or rebuilding several of Gresley's classic designs, sometimes for personal as

LNER Shire Class locomotive, number 265, *Lanarkshire*, designed by Nigel Gresley and built in 1927. Photographed in the 1930s.

The LNER's wagon building works at Faverdale, near Darlington in the 1930s, when up to 200 wagons were built each week.

well as technical reasons, and for his intolerance and short temper, Thompson nonetheless produced some successful locomotive classes for the LNER, notably the B1; more importantly, he saw the company through the dangers and

difficulties of the Second World War. He also designed the LNER's first generation of steel-bodied carriages.

Following Edward Thompson's retirement, Arthur Peppercorn became the LNER's last Chief Mechanical Engineer. Having been an apprentice under Gresley at the Great Northern Railway from 1905, Peppercorn knew him well and they became good friends as Gresley encouraged him in his career. So, when he was appointed in July 1946, he tended to support Gresley's ideas at the expense of Thompson's. Nevertheless, he was a sound and practical man who in his short reign as the LNER's Chief Mechanical Engineer produced some classic locomotive classes, notably the rebuilt A1 and A2 and the K1, which were seen as some of the best British steam locomotives of their time, powerful, reliable and modern in their design and construction. Although Arthur Peppercorn ceased to be the LNER's Chief Mechanical Engineer with the formation of nationalised British Railways, in effect he kept his job as he was appointed the Chief Mechanical Engineer for the newly formed Eastern and North Eastern Region of

Sir Nigel Gresley, Chief Mechanical Engineer of the LNER, 1923–1941.

LNER Class A3 number 4472, *Flying Scotsman*, designed by Nigel Gresley and built in 1923, and now back in service following a major rebuild.

B1 locomotive, from a class designed for the LNER by Edward Thompson in 1942. This example, number 61279, seen leaving Colchester in 1959, was built for British Railways in 1948.

British Railways and, until his retirement at the end of 1949, he oversaw the construction and operation by British Railways of the locomotive classes he had designed for the LNER.

At its formation, the LNER had to evaluate all the types of locomotive that had been inherited from the various constituent companies. Among the most modern and highly regarded were those built recently for the North Eastern Railway, to designs by Sir Vincent Raven, and for the Great Central Railway, designed by John G. Robinson. In fact, Robinson was offered the post of Chief Mechanical Engineer for the new LNER, but chose to step aside in favour of the younger Nigel

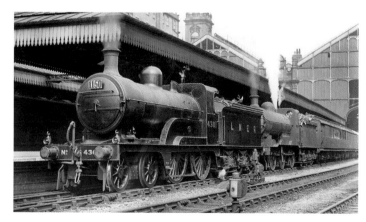

Former Great Northern Railway locomotives: Class D3 of 1897, in service with the LNER number 4301, and Class J6 of 1912 in service with the LNER number 3538, photographed at Nottingham Victoria with a Skegness to Leicester excursion in about 1936.

Gresley, who came to the LNER directly from the Great Northern Railway. As a result, Gresley was quickly able to develop his GNR designs further, creating a new generation of large, fast and impressive passenger locomotives for the LNER. However, he also made extensive use of ideas and technical advances made by his experienced predecessors such as Raven and Robinson.

All the LNER's inherited locomotives were classed according to their wheel configuration and renumbered accordingly. Thus, 4-6-2 was Class A, 4-6-0 Class B, 4-4-2 Class C, 4-4-0 Class D, 2-4-0 Class E and so on. Many subsequent letters were applied to minor and little-used wheel configurations, but some were important, such as Class J (0-6-0), Class K (2-6-0) and Class Q (0-8-0).

On the non-stop London to Edinburgh service the tenders had a corridor so that the second crew could travel in the first carriage and then move forward to the footplate to take over.

At the GNR, Gresley had favoured the 4-6-2, or Pacific, wheel configuration for his new express locomotives, and so he took this idea to the LNER, with the result that the LNER became the major user of the Pacific type among the Big Four until 1933 when the LMS introduced its first Pacific class. When British Railways took over on 1 January 1948, it inherited nearly 140 Pacific express locomotives from the LNER, and then built over 60 more to LNER designs. This seems relatively insignificant in the grand total of over 6,000 LNER locomotives handed over to British Railways, but included among them were all the LNER's most famous locomotives, including *Flying Scotsman* and *Mallard*. From the start, the LNER was very publicity conscious and made the most of the great public impact enjoyed by Gresley's new, green-painted locomotive classes on the East Coast main-line route between London and Edinburgh. They were large, impressive, efficient and reliable, and soon became well known for their high speeds. They could haul fully laden trains at speeds above 100mph, and they could run non-stop between London and Scotland.

THE A1, A2 AND A3 CLASSES

In April 1922, *Great Northern*, the first of a new class of Pacific express locomotive designed by Nigel Gresley, went into service on the Great Northern Railway. Three months later, a second one followed and a batch of nine was then ordered. These were designed to haul 600-ton trains and were soon proving they could do it. At exactly the same time, Sir Vincent Raven designed a similar Pacific passenger locomotive for the North Eastern Railway, and the first two of these were rushed into service. When the LNER took over, the rival locomotives were given A1 and A2 class designations and Gresley ran comparative tests between the two, which proved to him that his A1 design was the better, and so this became the LNER's major new express locomotive class. Over the next few years, progressive improvements were made, and from 1927 the A1s were given new boilers with a higher operating pressure, along with other refinements and these were given the A3 classification. Gradually all the A1s were rebuilt as A3s, with the last one being completed in 1947. In the end, there were eighty in the class and, with one exception, *Flying Scotsman*, they were all given the names of famous racehorses. All passed into British Railways in 1948. The survivor from the class is *Flying Scotsman*, probably the most famous locomotive in the world.

After Gresley's death Edward Thompson made further changes, with complicated re-classifications as A1/1, A2/1, A2/2 and A2/3, and with the ultimate aim of designing a new standardised replacement for the A class. This never got

beyond the drawing board but when Arthur Peppercorn took over he quickly brought it to life, and the first new A1 entered service in 1948, with another forty-eight quickly following. Peppercorn also inherited Thompson's final design, the A2/3, of which fifteen had been ordered. He then extensively modified the design and launched it as a new A2, which also came into service in 1948. The A1s carried an eclectic list of names, including racehorses, famous people (including famous locomotive engineers), characters and places from Walter Scott, pre-Grouping railway companies, seabirds and Scottish place names. In 2009 the fiftieth in the class, *Tornado*, went into service, having been built from scratch by the A1 Locomotive Trust, as none of the original A1s had survived into preservation. With one exception, the new A2s were named after racehorses, the exception being the first, which carried the name *A.H. Peppercorn*. However this, despite its importance, did not survive, and the only example of the class still in existence is *Blue Peter*.

The Class A1 locomotive, designed for the LNER by Arthur Peppercorn, enjoyed a long service with British Railways but none survived into preservation. So, in 2008 a new A1, number 60163, *Tornado*, was completed.

THE A4 CLASS

There is no doubt that the LNER's most famous, and most distinctive locomotive class is the streamlined A4. During the 1930s, railways were experiencing increasing competition from road and air travel, and so both the LNER and the LMS

LNER Class A4 locomotive number 4468, *Mallard*, designed by Nigel Gresley and the holder of the world speed record for steam locomotives since 1938.

set out to establish new standards of speed, reliability, luxury and comfort on the major routes between London, the north of England and Scotland. There was also the challenge from high-speed German and American trains, the 'Burlington Zephyr', for example, which was able to reach up to 112mph by 1934. Gresley therefore organised some high-speed runs with existing A1 and A3 locomotives, with *Papyrus*, one of the latter, setting a British record at 108mph, while hauling a much heavier train than the German and American record breakers.

With the LNER Board behind him, Gresley set out to create a brand new modern high-speed train, the 'Silver Jubilee', named to commemorate George V's Silver Jubilee in 1935. It was completely streamlined, from the wedge-shaped locomotive to the articulated carriages with valences between the bogies. The design was wind tunnel tested and it was established that at high speeds the streamlining was effective. In its silver and grey livery it also looked exciting and modern, and so the LNER's publicity made the most of it. During a demonstration run in September 1935 a speed of 112.5mph was recorded and a few days later the 'Silver Jubilee' went into

service, cutting the journey time from London to Newcastle to 4 hours. It was a great success and services were quickly extended. Meanwhile, on the other side of the country, the LMS was also operating its streamlined 'Coronation Scot' service on the West Coast main line.

Thus, by the latter part of the 1930s Britain had a high-speed rail network that was also safe, reliable and comfortable. At the same time, competition between the LNER and the LMS became more intense. On 28 June 1937 an LMS 'Coronation Scot' reached 114mph. On 3 July 1938 the LNER replied with a special train headed by a new A4, *Mallard*, and this was recorded at a peak average speed of 125mph over the measured section. This established a new world record for steam traction, and today, eighty years later, that world record still stands. In the 1930s garter blue and green liveries were

Two famous locomotives together, the preserved GNR Stirling Single, No. 1 of 1870 and Gresley A4 number 4498, *Sir Nigel Gresley*, photographed in about 1946.

The interior of the dynamometer carriage used on *Mallard*'s world record run, showing the speed recording equipment.

also used, while during the war the A4s were painted black, returning to a deeper blue after the war. The first four A4s had silver in their names, to haul the 'Silver Jubilee'. The remainder had bird names, names of major colonies and names of LNER directors and other important people.

With one exception (*Sir Ralph Wedgwood*, destroyed by bombing), all thirty-five A4s were transferred to British Railways and several continued to earn their keep until the end of steam. Six A4 locomotives have been preserved, including *Mallard*.

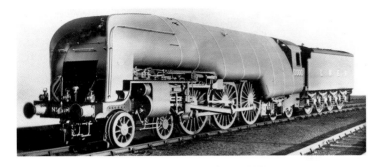

Postcard depicting the LNER Class W1 'Hush-Hush' high pressure locomotive 'No. 10,000', designed by Nigel Gresley and built in 1929.

THE W1 CLASS

In the mid-1920s Gresley attempted to apply the principles of high-pressure steam used by marine steam engines and so designed a locomotive around a high-pressure water tube boiler. This experimental locomotive, known as 'No. 10,000', and unofficially as 'Hush-Hush', was completed in 1929. With its size, rounded shape and 4-6-4 wheel configuration, the locomotive was immediately distinctive. In engineering terms, the working pressure of 450 pounds per square inch, combined with a compound cylinder arrangement, made it unique. During several years of service trials, the locomotive never really fulfilled its promise, despite constant modifications, and in 1936 it was re-boilered and rebuilt as a streamlined A4, while retaining its original wheel configuration. In this format it passed into British Railways and continued in service until it was scrapped in 1959. 'No. 10,000' represented an important attempt at pushing through the existing boundaries of steam locomotive engineering and, as with so many similar experiments, it was probably ahead of its time.

OTHER IMPORTANT LOCOMOTIVE CLASSES

A number of large tank engine classes were developed by Gresley for mixed traffic, freight and suburban uses, the most important being the 2-6-2 V1 and V3 classes. These

were introduced from 1930 and a total of ninety-two were built. Even more famous was Gresley's V2 class, the LNER's most successful mixed traffic design, and the tender version of the 2-6-2 tank locomotive. A total of 184 were built between 1936 and

LNER Class EM1 electric locomotive built in 1941 and designed for the Woodhead route. This photograph shows it in service with Dutch Railways in 1948.

1944. Another important Gresley design was the B17 Class of 4-6-0 passenger locomotives. Based on the heavier B12 class inherited from the Great Eastern Railway, these were known as 'Sandringhams' or 'Footballers', owing to their being named after East Anglian towns and British football clubs. A total of seventy-three were built between 1928 and 1937. Edward Thompson's most successful LNER design was the 4-6-0 Class B1, introduced in 1942 for mixed traffic work. Simple in design and relatively cheap to build, these two-cylinder locomotives were Thompson's response to what he saw as Gresley's overcomplicated engineering. A total of 410 were built between 1942 and 1952.

Among the locomotives inherited by the LNER were the 131 Class 8K 2-8-0 freight locomotives built by the Great Central Railway from 1911. These were re-classified by the LNER as O4, and the class was expanded with some modifications to 329, becoming one of the LNER's standard heavy freight locomotives, which also gave sterling service during the Second World War, at home and overseas. By far the most numerous locomotive type in Britain was the 0-6-0 in tender or tank form, designed for freight, branch line and shunting duties. At its formation, the LNER inherited over 2,500 of these from several constituent companies, notably the NER and the GNR, and went on to build 337 more. In 1915 the Great Eastern Railway had introduced a new class of L7 0-6-2 tank locomotives designed specifically for use on suburban services. These were very efficient and so Gresley re-classified the 134 he had inherited as the N7, and then arranged for a further 112 to be built between 1925 and 1928.

ELECTRIC TRAINS

In 1904 the North Eastern Railway started an electrified suburban network in the Tyneside region, initially with fifty-six powered cars and forty-four trailers, painted red and cream. As the routes were expanded, so more vehicles were built between 1908 and 1915. After a depot fire had destroyed thirty-four cars, replacements were built in 1920. In 1923 the LNER inherited the network and continued to operate it with the original vehicles until 1937, when the whole fleet was replaced with sixty-four new twin-car articulated sets. These remained in service until the 1960s.

The NER was also interested in electric locomotives and developed a variety of types between 1905 and 1922, mostly for freight use. Many were inherited by the LNER, with most surviving into the British Railways era. One of Gresley's last designs was for the EM1 class of electric locomotives, built specifically for the Woodhead route between Manchester and Sheffield. The first was completed in 1941, and formed the basis for British Railways Class 76 locomotives, in use until the early 1980s. The LNER EM1 class was also tried out by Dutch Railways in 1948.

The LNER also operated one tramway system, built originally by the Great Central Railway to link Grimsby and Immingham, and opened in 1913. This was operated throughout the LNER era and was finally closed in 1961.

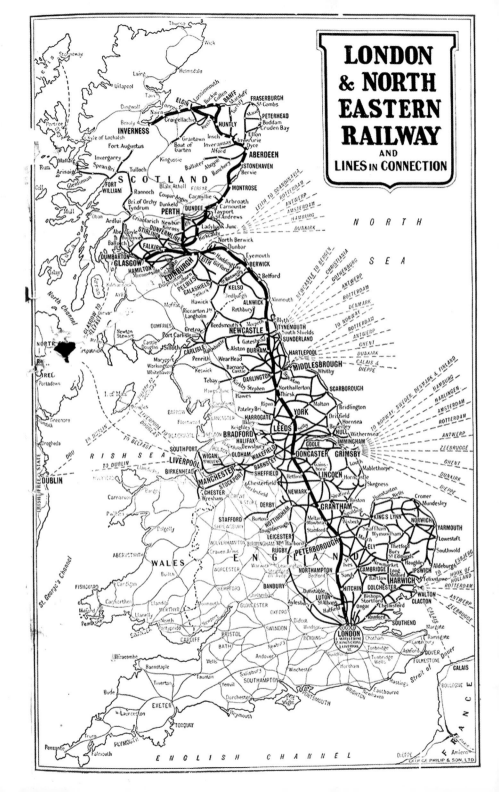

LONDON & NORTH EASTERN RAILWAY
AND
LINES IN CONNECTION

PASSENGER SERVICES

A TYPICAL LNER ROUTE map reveals the company's core passenger routes, at the heart of which is the East Coast main line from King's Cross to Edinburgh and thence to Dundee and Aberdeen, via Peterborough, Grantham, Doncaster, Darlington, York and Newcastle, along with the alternative route via Harrogate and Leeds. This was always the primary route in terms of investment and marketing and it was this route that created the LNER's reputation for speed, comfort and luxury. This was linked to major east-coast destinations such as Grimsby, Hull, Scarborough, Middlesbrough and Sunderland, and westwards to Manchester, Carlisle, Glasgow and Fort William. Also important was the former Great Central route from Marylebone to Sheffield via Rugby, Leicester and Nottingham. The LNER also controlled East Anglia and Lincolnshire, with its then dense network of main lines to Harwich, Cambridge, King's Lynn, Norwich, Yarmouth, Lowestoft and Lincoln. Connecting all this together is a mass of secondary routes, rural railways and branch lines, many of which were more important for freight rather than passenger traffic.

In its publicity, particularly its posters, the LNER made much of the numerous holiday resorts and regions it served, for example Clacton, Yarmouth, Cromer, Hunstanton, Skegness, Cleethorpes, Bridlington, Scarborough, Whitby, Saltburn, Redcar, Berwick and St Andrews, along with the moors and dales of Yorkshire, Durham and Northumberland. It was also

LNER network map showing primary and secondary routes, and connections with other companies and shipping services.

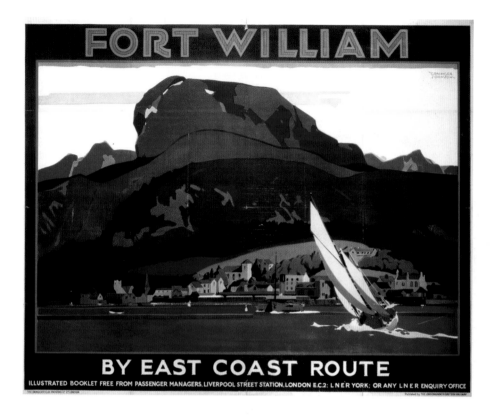

LNER poster promoting the East Coast route to Fort William and Western Scotland, from a painting by Grainger Johnson, 1923.

able to promote, through its connecting services and through carriage routes over other railways, predominantly the LMS, the Lancashire coast, North Wales, the Lake District, the Scottish Borders and the Highlands. There were also many famously scenic routes, for example on the former Midland and Great Northern Junction network around Norfolk, cross-country from Darlington to Penrith and from Newcastle to Carlisle, along the coast from Scarborough to Whitby and Middlesbrough, through the Borders from Alnwick to Melrose and Berwick, and from Glasgow to Fort William and Mallaig and all around the north-east of Scotland on the mostly rural network north of Aberdeen. Also promoted were great cathedrals and abbeys, famous cities and places of historical importance.

YORKSHIRE COAST NEAR WHITBY
IT'S QUICKER BY RAIL
FULL INFORMATION FROM ANY L·N·E·R OFFICE OR AGENCY

The same map indicates the complexity of passenger services the LNER was compelled to operate throughout its network of main lines and secondary routes. Although the LNER had inherited thousands of carriages from the various constituent companies, many of which remained in use over a surprisingly long period, particularly on minor and rural routes, high on the list of Nigel Gresley's priorities was the production of a standard corridor coach for the LNER main-line network. The design, a standard 60ft teak-panelled carriage, was finalised in 1923 and quickly put into production, and this remained the core of the LNER's carriage stock until 1942, when a new standard design by Edward Thompson went into production. Gresley was also famous for his articulated carriage sets, the first of which he had designed for the GNR in 1907, and so

LNER poster promoting travel along the Yorkshire Coast by train, from a painting by Frank Mason, 1937.

ELY

IT'S QUICKER BY RAIL

ILLUSTRATED BOOKLET FREE FROM L·N·E·R OFFICES AND AGENCIES
OR INFORMATION BUREAU, I MINSTER PLACE, ELY, CAMBRIDGESHIRE

JARROLD & SONS, LTD, NORWICH & LONDON   Printed in Great Britain   1940   Published by the LONDON & NORTH EASTERN RAILWAY he was able to build on this experience at the LNER.

At the same time, the LNER ran a very dense and busy suburban network. Much of this had been inherited from the Great Eastern, whose suburban services in and out of Liverpool Street were famously challenging and efficient. The GER's

LNER cinema car, 1930s, used on the 'Flying Scotsman' and other long-distance expresses.

suburban services were known as 'Jazz' trains, not because of their rapid turnaround at the start and end of each journey, but because of the coloured stripes on the carriages – yellow for 1st class, blue for 2nd – which gave the trains a jazzy appearance. However, there was much more, with the LNER's suburban traffic active in a semicircle to the north of London, from Clacton, Colchester, Chelmsford, Bishop's Stortford, Cambridge and Hitchin to Aylesbury. These services were operated generally by specially designed carriages in quadruplet sets that would be permanently coupled in pairs, to make the famous LNER eight-carriage sets known popularly as 'Quad-Arts'. These were built in large numbers in the 1920s, and continued to serve the main suburban routes well into the British Railways era. For other suburban routes, five-carriage quintuplet sets were also produced. These could also be paired to make ten-coach trains.

NAMED TRAINS

From the 1920s it became fashionable for major railway passenger routes to be given names, reflecting the destination. All the Big Four companies adopted this practice, mainly for marketing reasons, giving names to important passenger services leaving from London termini. The LNER had fewer

OPPOSITE
LNER poster featuring a painting of Ely and its cathedral by Edward Loxton Knight, 1930s.

A stopping service on the Bishop's Stortford to Braintree line pauses at Takeley Station in the 1930s, hauled by a former Great Eastern Railway tank locomotive.

named trains than its rivals and most related to services to Yorkshire, East Anglia and Scotland. The best known, and the oldest, is the 'Flying Scotsman', a service started in 1862 jointly by the NBR, the NER and the GNR. The name, widely used but informal, was officially established in 1924 by the LNER. Another early service was the 'Fifeshire Coast Express', set up by the NBR in 1912, and then operated by the LNER from 1923 to 1939. Other LNER named trains serving Scotland, and usually connecting London and Edinburgh, include the 'Coronation' and the 'Silver Jubilee', both in operation from the mid-1930s to 1939, the 'Night Scotsman', running during the 1930s, the 'Queen of Scots', a service from London to Glasgow in operation between 1927 and 1939 and the 'Highlandman', a 1930s service to Perth, Fort William and Inverness.

Promotional photograph for LNER's sleeper services, 1930s.

Postcard
depicting the
'Silver Jubilee',
1937.

The major destination for East Anglian named trains was Harwich, and these, the 'Antwerp Continental', the 'Day Continental' and, most famously, the 'Hook Continental', in operation from 1927 to 1939 and from 1945 to 1947, were boat trains. There were two other services, the 'East Anglian' to Norwich, established in 1937, and the 'Eastern Belle', a Pullman train to Clacton-on-Sea which operated

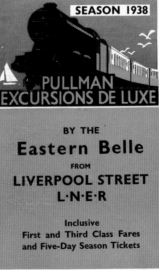

FAR LEFT
LNER brochure
promoting the
'Coronation', the
first streamlined
train, 1938.

LEFT
LNER folder
promoting the
'Eastern Belle'
Pullman service,
1938.

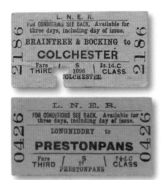

between 1929 and 1939. Another Pullman service set up in 1923 was the 'Harrogate Pullman' which was renamed the 'West Riding Pullman' in 1928 and was then run by the LNER until 1947. The route overlapped with the 'Yorkshire Pullman', from 1935 to 1939. Finally, the 'Master Cutler', a famous service to Sheffield, was established by the LNER in 1947, and then promptly taken over and further expanded by British Railways.

LNER tickets.

LNER BRANCH LINES

The route map also shows the many branch lines that became part of the large LNER network in 1923. These, spread all over the map, had varied histories. Some had been built by independent companies for local needs, and then later absorbed by bigger companies such as the GER, NER or GNR. Some were part of the busy suburban network, while others had a quiet life in remote areas, surviving largely from local freight carrying. A few connected popular tourist and holiday destinations to the main network, while others had been built from the late 1890s, following the passage of the Light Railway Act. Most were operated by 0-6-0 tender or tank locomotives hauling two or three elderly carriages, while some had two-carriage push-pull units. On a few, single-carriage steam railmotors had been tried out, often with limited success. For example, the GNR had built eight in 1905, six of which were taken over by the LNER, remaining in use until the Second World War. After trials with a prototype of a new design with high-speed steam engines and

LNER Sentinel steam railcar number 31, *Flower of Yarrow*, photographed in Carlisle Station in the 1930s.

Allendale Station was at the end of a 12-mile branch from Hexham. Little used, it was closed to passengers by the LNER in 1930 and to freight in 1950. This photograph shows the station in the late 1930s.

geared drive developed by Sentinel and Clayton, shown at the Wembley Exhibition in 1924, the LNER ordered eighty of these railmotors, and some of these were still in service in 1947. The LNER also inherited from the NER some petrol and petrol-electric railcars, but these had very limited use.

The LNER inherited around fifty branch lines and light railways, and it quickly realised that many of them were uneconomic because of under use and increased competition from road transport, particularly with regard to passenger traffic. They varied greatly in length and ranged from Essex to the north of Scotland. Among those in the former GER network were branches serving Ongar, Buntingford, Tollesbury, Hadleigh Eye, Framlingham, Aldeburgh, Laxfield

The Thaxted branch in Essex opened in 1913 and closed in 1953. One of the intermediate stations was Henham, where the station building was a retired railway carriage.

LNER first-class smoking compartment, 1930s.

(the former East Suffolk Light Railway), Mildenhall, Stoke Ferry, North Ramsey and East Ramsey. Northern branches absorbed mostly from the GNR and the NER included Withernsea, Hornsea, Pateley Bridge, Cawood, Masham, Middleton-in-Teesdale, Allendale, Alston and Rothbury, while in Scotland the list included Lauder, Gifford, Haddington, Gullane, Ballater, Alford, Old Meldrum, Boddam, St Combs and Lossiemouth. A number of these, notably those serving coalfields and other industrial locations, were busy freight lines but passenger carrying had always been of lesser importance and so the LNER began to withdraw passenger services on a number of branches. Among the first were the North Lindsay Light Railway and the Macmerry branch, both closed to passengers in 1925. Others followed in 1929, including Cawood, Ponteland and Carmellie, and then in the 1930s the closure programme increased, with the Hadleigh, Eye,

LNER buffet car for the 'Flying Scotsman', 1938.

FAR LEFT
Typical LNER
excursions
leaflet, 1920s.

LEFT
LNER Day Trips
and Hikes folder,
1938.

Masham, Stoke Ferry, Allendale, Amble, Gifford, Gullane, Lauder, Leslie, Bankfoot, Fort Augustus, Fochabers Town and Boddam branches losing passenger trains between 1930 and 1933, along with the Axholme Light Railway. Among the last to go in the LNER era were Spilsby in 1939, and North Ramsey in 1947. In all cases the branches were kept open for freight, with many surviving as freight-only lines until the 1960s.

EXCURSIONS AND HOLIDAYS

Britain's railway companies had established in the mid-Victorian period the habit of running excursion services as a way of maximising income and earning revenue from stock that might otherwise have been sitting in sidings and sheds and the practice was well established in most of the LNER's constituent companies. It was, therefore, relatively easy for the LNER to take over and develop further the excursion business, on both local and national levels. Excursions were widely promoted, and were seen as a way of familiarising the

LNER luggage labels.

Snow clearing in Belah Cutting between Barras and Bowes on the LNER's Darlington to Kirkby Stephen trans-Pennine route, 1930s.

travelling public with the LNER's new image, and the services it offered. Leaflets, brochures, guidebooks and posters were widely used, along with special ticket offers as the company steadily developed its holiday traffic. These were available from station ticket offices, and from travel agents, some of whom were either owned by, or had partnership agreements with, the LNER. By careful marketing, excursions could be offered throughout the year, thereby expanding the traditional holiday season, and throughout the network and into Europe via the company's ferry services. Excursions were also aimed at every level of the market, from trips and tours on luxury trains to seaside visits for factory workers during weekends and wakes weeks. Special interests were catered for, such as golf, fishing, horse racing, walking, theatre, music and ballet. Particularly well catered for were pigeon fanciers, as the LNER built a fleet of special pigeon carriers.

Also popular, particularly in the 1930s, were camping and walking and, along with the other Big Four the LNER produced leaflets, brochures and holiday guides aimed at campers and others keen on the outdoor life. This coincided with the rise of the holiday camp, whose growth and popularity from the

1930s was greatly helped by close railway connections. Some of the earliest holiday camps were on the Norfolk coast, at Caister and Hopton-on-Sea, and so the LNER was able to take over and expand the railway links. The first Butlin's holiday camp was opened in Skegness in 1936, and once again the LNER played its part in the success of this new venture. A second camp was opened at Clacton in 1938, and the building of a third, at Filey, was interrupted by the war. The holiday camp business expanded massively in the late 1940s and 1950s, by which time British Railways had taken over.

It was the LNER that came up with a novel idea to attract the camping and cheap holiday market when it launched the first camping coaches in 1933. Ten were sited in various locations in Northumberland, the Esk Valley, the Pennines and the Cheviots. The concept of parking old carriages adapted for family holidays on remote sidings at stations in rural, coastal and scenic locations was an immediate success, and the LMS, GWR and SR quickly followed the LNER's lead. By 1935, 215 camping coaches were established in 162 sites all over Britain. By 1938 the LNER

Washing day at an LNER camping coach near Southminster in Essex in 1935.

BUTLIN'S HOLIDAY CAMP
CLACTON-ON-SEA
IT'S QUICKER BY RAIL
ILLUSTRATED BOOKLET FREE FROM R. P. BUTLIN'S PUBLICITY DEPARTMENT, SKEGNESS, OR ANY L·N·E·R OFFICE OR AGENCY

LNER poster promoting Butlin's Holiday Camp at Clacton-on-Sea in Essex, from a painting by Joseph Greenup, 1938.

ABOVE LEFT
LNER folder
promoting
monthly return
tickets, 1936.

ABOVE RIGHT
LNER carriage
window labels.

had 119 coaches scattered around its network. Another LNER idea, launched in 1935, was a touring camping coach which could move round a pre-determined route by being attached to passenger trains. At the same time the LNER developed a series of camping apartments, adapted from redundant buildings at attractive station sites. Four were launched in 1935 but the idea did not catch on in the same way, not helped by some of them being on lines from which passenger services had been

The 'Queen
of Scots'
Pullman service,
introduced by
the LNER in
1927, prepares
to leave King's
Cross.

Newcastle Station, seen here in the 1930s, was famous for its signal gantry and the complexity of the track layout.

withdrawn. LNER's final contribution to the holiday trade was the 'Northern Belle', a Pullman cruise train which was, in effect, a five-star hotel on wheels that spent a week touring the company's network in the North and Scotland. In June 1936, the 'Belle' completed four tours. At the same time a far cheaper version, marketed as the 'Train Cruise', was aimed at scouts and other similar groups wanting to enjoy a much more basic railway tour. This cost 5 guineas per person, whereas the 'Northern Belle' cost £20.

LNER STATIONS

Virtually all the stations operated by the LNER, from major city termini to remote branch line halts, were built by the various constituent companies and their predecessors. Only a handful of new stations were opened by the LNER and these were all quite minor. Having been built by many different companies over a very long period, these stations were very diverse in appearance and so the LNER worked hard from 1924 to develop a standard

Postcard from 1908 depicting the GNR's Station Hotel in York, later taken over by the LNER and renamed the Royal Station Hotel.

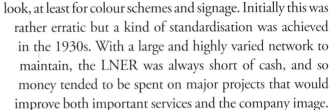

LNER luggage label for the Royal Station Hotel, York.

During the 1920s and 1930s railway hotels and their restaurants maintained a high standard and a reputation for elegance and luxury. This is the buffet at the former North British Hotel in Edinburgh in 1930.

look, at least for colour schemes and signage. Initially this was rather erratic but a kind of standardisation was achieved in the 1930s. With a large and highly varied network to maintain, the LNER was always short of cash, and so money tended to be spent on major projects that would improve both important services and the company image.

The great stations were the obvious ones, such as the London termini, York, Newcastle, Edinburgh, Perth, Aberdeen, Hull, Norwich and a number of others, many of which dated back to the early decades of Britain's railway history. Among the most modern inherited by the LNER were those along the former Great Central's main line from Marylebone, which had opened in 1899 with a series of new stations in Midland and Northern towns and cities.

LNER HOTELS

At the 1923 Grouping the LNER and the LMS became the largest operators of railway hotels, with the LNER inheriting around twenty from the constituent companies. The portfolio included a mix of business and holiday hotels, but the former were dominant, with grand Victorian station hotels at King's Cross and Liverpool Street in London, along with others at Peterborough, Harwich, Leeds, Bradford, Sheffield, York, West Hartlepool, Grimsby, Hull, Newcastle, Edinburgh, Glasgow and Aberdeen. Many of these were famous hotels made more successful by 1920s and 1930s modernisation. There were holiday hotels at Felixstowe, Hunstanton and Saltburn, along with the extraordinary Cruden Bay Hotel at Port Erroll on the east coast of Scotland, which had its own electric tram to transport guests and their luggage from the station. In 1948 the Hotels Executive, part of the new British Railways, took over seventeen former LNER hotels.

FREIGHT TRAFFIC

A T ITS FORMATION, the LNER inherited a vast and complex freight business that accounted for two-thirds of its revenues. The network served major areas of industry, for example coalfields in the Midlands, the North, the North East and Scotland, making the LNER one of Britain's largest coal carriers, both for industrial and domestic use, and for export. It also served the heavy engineering and shipbuilding centres of the North East, along with some of Britain's major fishing ports (Lowestoft, Yarmouth, Grimsby, Hull, Aberdeen, Peterhead and Fraserburgh) and the manufacturing centres of the Midlands and Yorkshire. It was a major carrier

A former Great Central Railway Class Q4 0-8-0 locomotive hauls a line of empty coal wagons through Nottingham Victoria while in the service of the LNER in about 1930.

Pig carcasses being unloaded from an insulated LNER container, carried by rail and then transferred to a flatbed lorry.

of agricultural materials, including potatoes, peas, fruit and other crops, foodstuffs of all kind, from ingredients to processed products, livestock, including racehorses, grain, hay and straw, cut flowers, fertilisers and much else besides.

Bulk freight apart, the LNER, like the other Big Four, operated a massive and integrated cargo carrying business that connected every station and goods depot in the network, transporting everything essential to the running of what was then a normal business and domestic life. In the 1920s, competition from road transport was still a distant, though growing threat, mostly kept at bay by railway companies operating their own fleets of lorries and horse-drawn vehicles for local deliveries and collections. By the 1930s this competition was much more severe, but the railways were to remain the dominant freight carrier until the 1950s. Along with their rivals, the LNER pioneered faster and more efficient transport systems, introducing containers that could move quickly from rail to road, backed up by other modern integrated freight handling

LNER cast-iron warning sign.

systems. A new generation of high-capacity freight vehicles was developed, while other improvements included better braking systems and more refrigerated vehicles for perishable traffic.

While the movement of massive quantities of coal remained the major revenue earner, the transport of small items from the manufacturer or wholesaler to a village shop at the end of a branch line remained an important part of the freight business through the LNER era. This was one of the main reasons why branch lines and country routes closed to passengers by the LNER remained open for freight traffic.

The LNER also operated at least twenty major dock complexes, all established by its constituent companies, and so were at the forefront of Britain's vital import and export business. These included Harwich Parkeston Quay, Grimsby, Hartlepool, Hull, Middlesbrough, Sunderland and those along the Tyne and the Wear, Leith, Dundee and Aberdeen. One of the most modern docks was Immingham, developed by the

ABOVE LEFT
A special LNER freight train transports castings for the new Cunard liner *Queen Mary* from Darlington to Middlesbrough in 1931.

ABOVE RIGHT
In what appears to be a classic LNER scene, a Thompson Class B1 locomotive hauls a mixed freight out of Perth and across the Tay. In fact, it is 1965, and steam is soon to disappear from Scotland.

Postcard depicting the *Talisman*, a diesel-electric paddle ship built for the LNER in 1935. From 1940 it became HMS *Aristocrat*.

LNER poster promoting the Harwich–Zeebrugge train ferry service, 1930s.

LNER wagon labels.

Great Central Railway and opened in 1912. Primarily built for the export of coal, its facilities could move 400 tons an hour. Other major cargoes included timber, pig iron and grain. Immingham was also equipped to handle passenger ships, and during the 1930s was used as a base for cruise ships.

Immingham was also a major LNER ferry port, with services to Norway, Sweden, Hamburg, Amsterdam and Rotterdam, Antwerp, Zeebrugge and Ghent, Dunkirk and Dieppe. The other ferry ports were Harwich, Hartlepool, Newcastle and Leith. Services were operated by many shipping lines, including the LNER's own ships. The fleet included over twenty ships, mostly inherited from the constituent companies. Some dated back to the 1890s but most were quite modern in 1923. The LNER also commissioned some new ships, the SS *Prague* and SS *Vienna* in 1929, the SS *Amsterdam* in 1930, the SS *Arnhem* in 1946, and the MV *Suffolk Ferry* in 1947. There were also three train ferries, built originally for service during the First World War and acquired by the LNER in 1923 to operate the freight-only Harwich–Zeebrugge route.

THE LNER AT WAR

Using an order issued under the umbrella of the Emergency Powers (Defence) Act of 1939, the government took control of the British railway network with effect from 1 September 1939. In the process the usual activities of the railways were immediately transferred from peacetime to wartime operating conditions. For the duration of this period of government control, which was planned to stay in place for at least a year after the cessation of hostilities, the Big Four and London Transport were to be given annual payments by the government as a kind of compensation. As the operator of one of the bigger networks, and therefore

A streamlined Class A4 locomotive, number 4469, was renamed *Sir Ralph Wedgwood* in March 1939 to mark his retirement after sixteen years at the helm of the LNER. In April 1942, while stabled overnight at York's North Shed, it was destroyed during a Baedeker bombing raid.

An LNER promotional photograph showing the blackout arrangements in a second-class compartment.

the greater potential loser, the LNER was to receive £10,136,355 per annum. To put this in context, the total main-line receipts in 1938 for Britain's railway companies was £159.7 million, a fall of 18 per cent from the Grouping in 1923 when the total had been £195.6 million. In fact, railway revenues had fallen steadily during the 1920s and 1930s, despite massive investments in new locomotives and rolling stock, and in track and infrastructure improvements.

The impact of the war was immediate. Despite restrictions on passenger travel (underlined by that famous slogan, 'Is your journey really necessary?'), railway traffic increased hugely. In 1942 passenger travel on the British main-line network totalled 30,000 million miles, a 50 per cent increase on the typical pre-war mileage. At the same time, there was a 28 per cent reduction in the mileage run by passenger trains, meaning that the loading of each train had more than doubled. Much of this, of course, represented the movement of military personnel. To give two examples, the short-lived Norway campaign in 1940 required the running of 202 special trains, while the preparations for the North African campaign in 1942 required 440 troop trains, 680 freight trains and 15,000 wagons moved by ordinary goods trains. This was a continuous and ever-expanding task, as the war drew in more and more soldiers, sailors, airmen and their support staff. Civilian movements were also important. The evacuation of children from London during the 1940 Blitz involved 4,349 special trains, carrying 1,428,425 people. And, strange though it may now seem, throughout the war people continued to go on holiday and to travel for all kinds of private reasons.

However, at the heart of the management of the war was the movement of freight, with a million loaded wagons being moved through the British network every week. Freight trains became longer and more frequent, and there were more and more special tasks, many involving the

construction of airfields, fortifications and factories. The rebuilding of one airfield to the size required by the US Army Air Force required the rapid delivery of 500,000 tons of cement. Coal remained the major cargo, with over 160,000,000 tons being moved every year, indicating that the production and distribution of coal was crucial to the war effort. Equally important was the transport of raw materials, components and completed equipment for the army, navy and air force, and linked to this was the ever-expanding number of factories, requiring the transport of building materials and equipment, all the support facilities, the movement of the workforce and the distribution of the finished products. One large factory required fifty-eight trains a day, with ten leaving within 20 minutes at the peak period.

During the Second World War, railway works were often turned over to the making of armaments, notably guns and tanks, and women frequently took over the skilled machining work, seen here at Doncaster in 1943.

The result of this massive expansion of rail traffic over the years of the war had a lasting impact, with locomotives and rolling stock working much harder with reduced maintenance. Track and infrastructure suffered in the same way. There were constant equipment failures, yet more and more trains were required. By 1943 the government realised that some standard locomotives were required, for use in Britain and overseas, and hundreds were built, based largely on the LMS 2-8-0 freight locomotive and the LNER 4-6-0 mixed traffic class and 0-8-0 shunting tanks. Soon, examples of these were at work through Britain, North Africa and the Middle East and they moved into Europe to support the invasion forces as they moved eastwards in 1944 and 1945.

However, by the end of the war the railways were in a parlous state, thanks to years of overuse and the maintenance backlog. To make matters worse, much of the network had been under constant attack from German bombers, one of whose major tasks was to try to close down the railway network. Stations, signal boxes, works, sheds, depots, warehouses, bridges and other structures and railway junctions were regularly attacked, but it was rare for services to be seriously interrupted for long. Repair gangs were constantly at work and, thanks to the dense intricacies of the British network, alternative routes could usually be found. Traditional boundaries between the Big Four were often abandoned, and so an LNER locomotive and crew could find itself working on the LMS, and vice versa. Keeping the system running was a constant challenge, made more difficult by the shortage of skilled railway managers, staff and crews as so many had been called up to serve in the forces. Women played a vital role in filling many of the gaps in all areas of railway activity, but they could not replace an experienced driver, or a manager with skills developed over years.

Throughout the war, the LNER experience was part of this. Serving as it did many of Britain's coalfields, and the great engineering and shipbuilding centres, it faced more demands than some other companies, and so its locomotives, rolling stock, infrastructure and staff were heavily challenged. It survived, as did the other companies but, when the war was over, it found it hard to get back to a pre-war way of working. In essence, everything was worn out and there was little money to rebuild the network. With the government still in control of the railways, and a new Labour party in power, the route to nationalisation seemed inevitable.

THE LNER LEGACY

O N 1 JANUARY 1948, British Railways took control of the national network; the Big Four, having survived the challenges of the war, ceased to exist. The LNER was split into three BR regions, Eastern, North Eastern and Scottish. Despite this, there was some continuity, as Arthur Peppercorn was appointed BR's Chief Mechanical Engineer for the Eastern and North Eastern Regions, and his major locomotive classes continued in production, along with Edward Thompson's B1. Meanwhile BR was extensively testing the very varied and distinctive locomotive types produced by the pre-war Big Four to establish the best design and manufacturing ideas for their forthcoming standard locomotive range. LNER and LMS locomotives played a crucial role in this.

The LNER lives on: in this photograph, a local passenger train passes through Saxmundham in the early 1950s; the locomotive was built for the Great Eastern Railway in 1911, served through the LNER era, and worked for British Railways until 1955.

Production continued at the former LNER locomotive works at Darlington, with two of British Railways' new standard-class locomotives under construction in 1956.

From the start, British Railways was keen to impose standardisation, in locomotives and rolling stock, in stations and buildings, in management processes and in branding and advertising. At the same time, traditional regional variations survived, and BR acknowledged this in many ways. Trains and operating procedures continued to reflect their pre-war owners, and staff frequently retained a regional loyalty. In the late 1940s British Railways formalised the BR brand and image, with a new style of universal signage for stations and buildings, and a new, related house style for publicity material. However, pre-war regional boundaries were acknowledged in the colours selected, with the obvious ones being Western Region brown and Southern Region green. The Eastern Region used an LNER blue, while the North East was orange and Scotland a paler, Caledonian blue. BR also brought back many of the LNER's famous pre-war named trains, such as the 'Flying Scotsman' and the 'Hook Continental', and added some new ones.

British Railways also maintained the spirit of competition that had defined the main-line relationship between the LMS and the LNER, particularly on routes to Scotland, a rivalry of course dating back to the Victorian era. As part of its 1955 modernisation plan, BR announced the electrification of the West Coast main line, and this project, starting in 1959, was completed in 1974. The resulting faster journey times, offered by a new generation of high-speed electric trains, cast a shadow over the East Coast main line, though the electrification of this between 1976 and 1991 restored the level playing field. Prior to electrification, BR had tended to favour the former LNER route to Scotland, by introducing onto it new locomotives and rolling stock as steam was gradually phased out. The end of steam had also been part of the 1955 modernisation plan and, while this took longer than planned, the end was in sight by the early 1960s. As it turned out, the last steam-hauled trains to run on the BR network in 1968 were in the North East region, on former LNER territory, a satisfactory conclusion in historical terms as the North East was the birthplace of Britain's railways.

In 1962 a gleaming new Deltic locomotive, having just been named *Royal Scots Grey*, prepares to haul the centenary 'Flying Scotsman' out of Edinburgh.

In 1961 British Railways introduced a new class of diesel locomotive onto the East Coast main line. These, known formally as Class 55s and informally as 'Deltics', after the Napier Deltic engine that powered them, had been specially designed for this route. Their impact was immediate as their great power steadily reduced the journey time between London and Edinburgh, and regularly achieved speeds of over 100mph. In all, twenty-two Deltics were built in 1961 and 1962, and they maintained LNER locomotive practice in carrying the names of racehorses, along with army regiments. They were magnificent machines and quickly achieved a popular following and impressive service records as they thundered between London and Edinburgh and London and Leeds. They dominated the former LNER main lines until the mid-1970s when they began to be replaced, and their special relationship with the LNER's primary route was widely seen as an acknowledgement of the importance and individuality of that company. This regionalism was not unique for, at the same time, individual and distinctive classes of diesel locomotives also ran on the Western and Southern regions of British Railways. By the 1970s BR management was imposing necessary standardisation on its locomotive fleet and these small classes of individual locomotives were withdrawn and replaced.

For the Deltics, the replacement was the BR Class 43, known as the 'Intercity 125', or the 'HST 125'. Designed to

With its elegant livery and concern for detail the GNER kept alive the spirit of the LNER on the East Coast main line. In this photograph a Class 91 electric locomotive heads its train across the Royal Border Bridge at Berwick.

have an operating speed of 125mph, hence the name, these represented a radical break from locomotive haulage. They were built as diesel multiple units, with a power car at each end, thereby greatly simplifying operations. The prototype quickly established the world record speed for a diesel train, at 143mph, and so BR's marketing department promoted them as the world's fastest diesel train. Introduced on the East Coast main line in 1976, these new trains spread quickly to other regions, and were soon seen as the modern image of BR on non-electrified routes. It is a mark of their design and engineering quality that the HST 125 is still widely used throughout the modern network.

When British Rail was destroyed and torn apart by the privatisation process, new train operators quickly took over the key routes. The former BR regions, and their links to the regions formed by the 1923 Grouping, disappeared. Most of the new operators and their trains ignored or abandoned hitherto important historical sources and connections. However, there was one important exception. The East Coast main line and other primary routes of the former LNER were taken over in April 1996 by Sea Containers, who had set up a number of luxury train services, notably the 'Venice Simplon Orient-Express'. They named their new train company the GNER, the Great North Eastern Railway. With a distinctive, elegant and quite traditional livery, and with a great concern for the design and appearance of every detail of the trains and the service that drew something from their luxury trains experience, GNER clearly and deliberately echoed the LNER. The carriages carried handsome, cast brass cresting, with some including the phrase 'The Route of the Flying Scotsman' and the train sets contained traditional dining cars. Until it lost the franchise in December 2007, the GNER and its classic trains kept alive the spirit of the old LNER, notably in King's Cross, York and Edinburgh and along the East Coast main line.

Knebworth Station in Hertfordshire reveals its history: a GNR station lamp from the 1890s, a British Railways totem name board from the 1950s and a porter in 1970s uniform struggling with the gas. The railings probably date from the LNER era.

The LNER legacy is also carried forward by the re-emergence into main-line and heritage service of the *Flying Scotsman*, following a massive and hugely expensive rebuild, and this has quickly become the world's most famous steam locomotive. The new Peppercorn A1, *Tornado*, completed in 2008, also flies the LNER flag, though it commemorates a very successful locomotive type from the early years of British Railways, and carries a BR number. Other new-build LNER locomotive types are in the pipeline.

Despite its short life of twenty-five years, the LNER represented an important, distinctive and memorable chapter in the long history of Britain's railway network. At its peak in the 1930s, it was the epitome of fast, stylish, luxurious, comfortable and safe railway travel, with services operated by some of Britain's most famous railway locomotives. Behind that famous façade was also Britain's major freight operator, a vital resource for British industry.

FURTHER READING

Adair, David. *Modellers' Guide to the LNER*. Patrick Stephens, 1987.

Bonavia, Michael. *A History of the LNER*. 3 vols: (1) The Early Years, 1923–33; (2) The Age of the Streamliners, 1934–39; (3) The Last Years, 1939–48. Allen & Unwin, from 1982.

Gammell, C.J. *LNER Branch Lines*. Oxford Publishing Company, 1993.

Harris, Michael. *LNER Carriages*. Crecy Publishing, 2011.

Hughes, Geoffrey. *LNER*. Ian Allan, 1986.

Tatlow, Peter. *A Pictorial Record of LNER Wagons*. Oxford Publishing Company, 1976.

Wethersett, R.R., and Asher, L.L. *Locomotives of the LNER: A Pictorial Record*. Heffer, 1947.

Whitehouse, Patrick, and Thomas, David St John. *LNER 150*. Guild Publishing, 1989.

Online resource: *The London and North Eastern Railway Encyclopedia* (www.lner.info). This covers all aspects of the LNER's history and includes a discussion forum.

LNER poster from a series produced by the LNER to promote its support for the industries of the east coast. Taken from a painting by Frank Mason, this depicts the coal industry, 1938.

EAST COAST INDUSTRIES
SERVED BY THE L·N·E·R

PLACES TO VISIT

Bressingham Steam & Gardens, Low Road, Bressingham, Diss, Norfolk IP22 2AA. Telephone: 01379 686900. Website: www.bressingham.co.uk

East Anglian Railway Museum, Station Road, Wakes Colne CO6 2DS. Telephone: 01206 242524. Website: www.earm.co.uk

Head of Steam (formerly Darlington Railway Museum), Station Road, Darlington DL3 6ST. Telephone: 01325 405060. Website: http://www.darlington.gov.uk/leisure-and-culture/head-of-steam/

Keighley & Worth Valley Railway, The Railway Station, Station Road, Haworth BD22 8NJ. Telephone: 01535 645214. Website: www.kwvr.co.uk

The National Railway Museum at Shildon, Dale Road Industrial Estate, Shildon DL4 2RE. Telephone: 01904 685780. Website: www.nrm.org.uk

North Norfolk Railway, Sheringham Station, Station Approach, Sheringham, Norfolk NR26 8RA. Telephone: 01263 820800. Website: http://www.nnrailway.co.uk

North York Moors Historical Railway Trust, Pickering Station, Pickering, North Yorkshire, YO18 7AJ. Telephone: 01751 473799. Website: www.nymr.co.uk

Riverside Museum (Scotland's museum of transport and travel), Pointhouse Place, Glasgow G3 8RS. Telephone: 0141 287 2720. Website: https://beta.glasgowlife.org.uk/museums/venues/riverside-museum

INDEX